THE PETER PRINCIPLE

Say NO! to incompetence at work

Written by Gabriel Verboomen
In collaboration with Brigitte Feys
Translated by Carly Probert

Business 50MINUTES.com

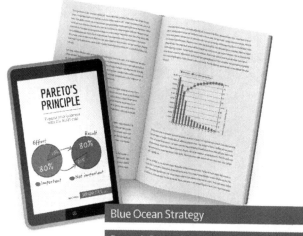

THE PETER PRINCIPLE

KEY INFORMATION

- **Name:** the Peter Principle.
- **Uses:** human resource and performance management, development of human potential.
- **Why is it successful?** Its success is uncertain because it depends on the individuals and the organisations.
- **Key words:**
  - <u>Competence:</u> knowledge and know-how required for maximum efficiency in a given position
  - <u>Efficiency:</u> synonymous with excellence, the ability of an employee to perform certain tasks with limited resources (time, money, etc.)
  - <u>Hierarchy:</u> authority structure within an organisation
  - <u>Promotion:</u> appointing a worker to a higher level within an organisation.

INTRODUCTION

When considering the Peter Principle, it is particularly important to realise that this model, though enlightening in many given situations, comes from a satirical book and, therefore, must be used with caution to when establishing scientific facts. In the context of increasingly strong hierarchies within organisations, there is the question of internal promotion. Should the competence of an employee be the dominant criterion for determining hierarchical ascension? How can this level of competence be measured? Does an efficient employee necessarily make for a good organiser?

DEFINITION OF THE MODEL

The Peter Principle states that if an employee is working efficiently at a given hierarchical level, he will be promoted to the next level above and so on, until he reaches the level where he is inefficient. If he cannot be demoted, this means that all structures naturally evolve towards a balance of greater inefficiency.

Although, at first glance, the principle may seem absurd, it does raise some issues regarding human resource management. Who should be promoted for the good of both the individual and the company? And under what conditions should this be done in order to increase overall efficiency?

THEORY

THE HYPOTHESES OF THE PETER PRINCIPLE

The Peter Principle, like all economic models, is based on hypotheses that are useful to investigate. If we only look at the most important, these include (but are not limited to):

- The hierarchical structure of a company is naturally in the form of a pyramid. This simplified view shows the strictly defined hierarchical levels: basic workers are led by a few managers, who are themselves managed by even fewer superior executives and so on.

The pyramid structure

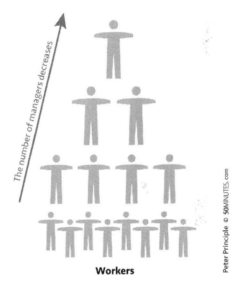

Workers

- Working positions are rigid and include set tasks: the worker assigned to a position performs a certain number of tasks. If he fails to do the work expected, it will simply not get done. If he succeeds, he will not be given other tasks. In this regard, however, note that these structural descriptions date back to a certain time and companies are currently much more flexible organisations that work from a project or network, for example.

- The strongest and most controversial hypothesis is what the book refers to as the 'Peter hypothesis'. The level of competence required for a higher hierarchical position is completely independent of the competence required for a hierarchically inferior position. If an employee is the most suitable for a position and is promoted to a higher level, his level of competence after that promotion is completely unpredictable.

According to Jean-Paul Delahaye (French computer scientist and mathematician, born in 1952), if we accept these simplistic assumptions, we are logically assuming that all promotions have a tendency to reduce an employee's performance due to two effects:

- **The ratchet effect:** backtracking is impossible as an employee cannot be demoted. If he is competitive, he will continue to climb the ladder and will not remain in a position where he is efficient. The movement will effectively continue until he reaches a level that is too high, in which he is no longer efficient. The employee is then stuck at this level and cannot be demoted nor continue to rise.
- **The statistical effect of regressing towards the average (of the principle of statistical distribution):** during a random, 'normal' event, the probability of achieving a result close to average is higher than getting a very high or very low result. Thus, the company, which is fortunate enough to be able to count on an employee that is well

above average competency and decides to change their position, once again determines the competence of the employee with a good chance of achieving an average result.

The Peter Principle

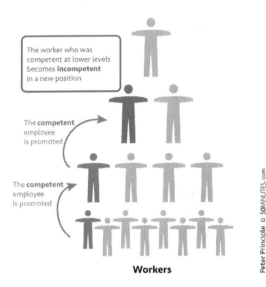

The worker who was competent at lower levels becomes **incompetent** in a new position

The **competent** employee is promoted

The **competent** employee is promoted

Workers

Peter Principle © 50MINUTES.com

Behind the hypotheses of the Peter Principle lies an inconvenient truth: over time, each position is increasingly likely to be occupied by an incompetent employee, while the higher up a position is in the hierarchy, the more important it is to the overall performance of the structure. This does not mean that the base of the pyramid is any less essential to the proper functioning of the business than the top, it is in fact the reverse. Put simply, if we accept the pyramid structure and place equal emphasis on each level, a position has more importance for the overall performance when there are fewer positions within that level. For example, if there are two managers for five employees, the individual competence of the manager accounts for 50% of the performance of its hierarchical level, while the individual performance of each employee only accounts for 20%.

In the hypotheses of the Peter Principle, particularly that of the ratchet effect, it seems clear that 'every employee tends to rise to his level of incompetence', so that the natural balance of a structure is that each position is occupied by someone who cannot bear the responsibilities.

THE INCOMPETENT EMPLOYEES

This principle was conceived by Laurence J. Peter as part of a complete science of organisations that he called 'hierarchiology'.

This seeks to provide concrete applications and confronts his model with the reality of the organisations that he observed. Of course, he notes exceptions to the principle. For example, the most competent are not always promoted. He highlights several cases where incompetent employees are promoted and explains why.

- **Powerful sublimation or pseudo-development:** this strategy, which promotes an incompetent employee to an upper level, mainly serves to maintain the hope of all others who believe they may also be promoted one day. This is dangerous because it is just an illusion for people who are not part of the hierarchy.

- **Lateral arabesque:** this promotes an incompetent employee to a new, useless position with a grander title to limit the damage he may cause in his current position.
- **Peter reversal:** in this case, the promotion of an incompetent employee is due to their compliance with standards imposed by the hierarchy rather than their efficiency. The end effect and means are reversed, since the standards exist to increase productivity and give as much value to compliance of standards as to productivity.
- **Hierarchical defoliation:** to avoid workers perceiving the absurdity of the system and deciding not to comply, the company favours the promotion of an incompetent employee.

SIGNS OF THE LAST POSITION

According to Peter, the signs of incompetence, or the signs of hiding incompetence from others and oneself, are easy to detect. These are called 'signs of the last position': however, they give the illusion of professional fulfilment.

- **Classophilia:** from the Greek word 'classis' (meaning 'category' or 'class'), this is an unnecessary obsession with classification to give (themselves) the illusion that they are doing important work.
- **Gigantism tabula:** refers to the incompetent employee who wants the biggest office.

- **Papyromania:** from the Greek word 'Papyros' ('paper') and the Latin word 'mania' ('madness' or 'obsession'), this is a sign of an incompetent employee who piles up paperwork – hence the apparent disorder – on his desk to give the impression that he is extremely busy.
- **Papyrophobia:** from the Greek words 'papyros' ('paper') and 'phobos' ('phobia'), is a sign of an incompetent employee who cannot tolerate any paper in their workspace. If the office is organised, colleagues, superiors, and perhaps even the employee himself, will believe that work is being done efficiently.
- **Phonophilia:** from the Greek words 'phone' ('voice') and 'philos' ('friend'), this is a sign of incompetence which involves blaming a lack of contact with colleagues and subordinates and installing multiple phones and tape recorders in the office. Since this idea first appeared in 1969, this 'sign' should probably be rephrased based on current technologies.
- **Rigor Cartis:** of Latin origin, this indicates an obsessive interest in graphics, diagrams and charts that give the illusion of control over situations.
- **Initial siglomania:** from the Latin words 'sigla' (meaning 'markings' or 'abbreviations') and 'mania' (meaning 'madness' or 'obsession'), this is a sign where the incompetent employee will speak using incomprehensible initials and acronyms with non-initiated staff, to give the impression of professionalism. He will complicate things as he takes pleasure in the importance this gives him.
- **Structurophilia:** from the Latin word 'structure' ('arrangement', 'construction') and the Greek 'philos' ('friend'), this involves enjoying work in a certain structure, the

incompetent employee that shows evidence of this sign will be obsessed with the order and maintenance of the building where he works, to the detriment of enjoying the work itself.

- **Flutter syndrome:** the incompetent employee rarely makes decisions and allows them to wait a long time before being processed.
- **Abnormal tabula:** from the Latin word 'tabula' ('plate' or 'table'), this is a sign of incompetence where the employee uses unusual and strange office equipment.

However, Peter qualifies his statements by explaining that, fortunately for the functioning of our political, social and economic models, all positions at the top of the hierarchy are not necessarily occupied by incompetent employees. In fact, in this clarification of the principle, he highlights the fact that the hierarchical structure of an organisation is often too small for all of the competent people – although this is not too big a fault, as otherwise they would suffer from hierarchical defoliation – to reach their potential. Nonetheless, note that the competent superiors are often headhunted by larger organisations where they are once again able to move up until they too reach their level of incompetence.

LIMITATIONS AND EXTENSIONS

LIMITATIONS AND CRITICISMS

The limits of the model are obvious as soon as one considers the hypotheses that it is based on.

- At the moment, an organisation is often not as simple as the pyramid structure described by Peter. Most of the time, an employee who coordinates others has not been promoted. The various departments are on equal footing, at least in theory. Decentralisation and empowerment are encouraged and there is a tendency to reduce the straightforward vertical hierarchy. This phenomenon is called 'the flattening of the pyramids'. Perhaps it is precisely one of the contemporary ways to avoid the effects of the Peter Principle which originate from a time when hierarchy was more rigid?
- A position is no longer frozen. If an incompetent employee is appointed to a position and does not assume its responsibilities, it is likely that many of the functions will be progressively assigned to another position.
- The issue of motivation is also problematic, since some skills shown by the worker can come from this. Indeed, the employee may be efficient at one level of the hierarchy, partially due to motivation. If he continues this enthusiasm he is likely to acquire the new skills required for the new position more easily, making him more efficient.
- The current realities of turnover are impressive, since it is estimated that a young person entering the labour market is likely to change their function or business

approximately five times.

- Finally, certainly the most questionable Peter hypothesis is that the competency shown in one position is inherently independent from the competency proved in a previous position. Other researchers, such as the Italian physicists Alessandro Pluchino, Andrea Rapisarda, and sociologist Cesare Garofalo in their article *The Peter Principle Revisited: A Computational Study*, offer a revisited perspective of the famous principle by stating the opposite hypothesis. They call it 'the common sense hypothesis': competency in a higher position depends on the competency shown in a lower position and is increased or decreased by approximately 10%.

The empirical testing of incompetence developed by Peter can also be unreliable. Indeed, the symptoms include so many different behaviours that we cannot, as some do, use them as supposed proof of the Peter Principle. If we consider the face value of certain hypotheses, we will eventually be confronted with situations such as this: the person who likes organisation too much or is too authoritative is incompetent, but the person who is not organised enough or is not authoritative is also incompetent. If excess is always a bad thing, the majority of the alleged symptoms can originally be perceived as qualities. Also, is it the reason why an incompetent employee adopts these attitudes – but to the extreme – to try to hide his incompetence. In conclusion, the Peter Principle is unverifiable and the satirical tone he uses in his work suggests that it has no real scientific claim.

RELATED MODELS AND EXTENSIONS

The Peter Principle is part of a set of 'laws' of the same type, of a more or less humorous style, which describe the corporate world with a certain cynicism and whose scientific rigour is not its biggest concern. However, some of them point out the challenging realities with which most organisations must effectively cope.

Parkinson's Law

Among these, in particular there is Parkinson's Law (1955), from the British historian Cyril Northcote Parkinson (1909-1993), which states that the work is always spread out in order to fill the time available to the person in charge of the work. By extension, we can imagine that all available resources for are project are used, whether they are time, money, manpower, etc. There are two consequences underpin this law:

- **Increase of subordinates.** If an employee fails to complete a project, he only has two options: he can either unload a portion of the work by giving it to someone who could become a potential rival, or he can request the support of his subordinates. In most cases, the second option is chosen, firstly to protect his position and secondly to increase his importance. It should be noted that he will ensure he has several subordinates, so as to share each task. That way, since none of them are able to perform the whole task, no one will become a potential rival.
- **Increase of workload.** Whether working with equals or subordinates, the fact is that when there are several

people working, the workload increases. It often takes as much time to coordinate the task as it does to do the work. As there is almost always someone in the team who has trouble delegating and takes on more responsibility, the work will rectify itself in the end to match what one person could have produced alone. Ultimately, to produce the same work – as only one person would have produced – it takes a whole team dedicated to it and additional time was spent coordinating all of these people.

The Dilbert Principle

We will also mention the Dilbert Principle, derived from an eponymous comic strip by Scott Adams (American cartoonist, born in 1957). According to him, the incompetent employees are immediately promoted and become managers, even if they have never shown any special skills. This principle is even more radical than the Peter Principle, since it assumes that we consciously entrust management functions to incompetent employees so that they cannot cause any damage. This, of course, assumes that management is always useless.

Comparison between the Peter Principle and the Dilbert Principle

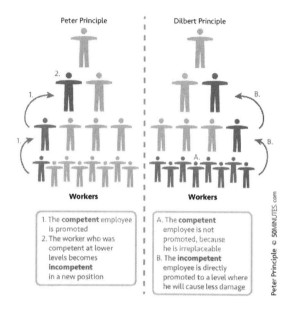

Peter Principle

Dilbert Principle

Workers

Workers

1. The **competent** employee is promoted
2. The worker who was competent at lower levels becomes **incompetent** in a new position

A. The **competent** employee is not promoted, because he is irreplaceable
B. The **incompetent** employee is directly promoted to a level where he will cause less damage

Peter Principle © 50MINUTES.com

Similarly, we can cite the popular saying that "those who can, do; those who can't, teach".

Although we cannot call them 'models' as such – because they are not scientific – these principles show some empirical resistance to the theoretical performance of economic models. Should we give up on these models – the limits of

which we know in reality – and consider granting promotions at random?

PRACTICAL APPLICATION

The case studies where the Peter Principle is at work are both numerous and non-existent at the same time. They are numerous, since each of us easily manages to imagine a situation where an incompetent employee is promoted, recognising the signs described by Peter among our colleagues or superiors. As for saying that they actually prove incompetence, that is another matter. It is quite difficult, and most human resource managers know this well, to measure the performance of an employee. Similarly, employees will often tend to find their superior incompetent because it is easier to criticise others than to take responsibility. Most of the time, literature presents cases where incompetence is claimed, but comes from little more than the imagination of Peter Principle supporters. In this sense, real case examples are non-existent.

STUDY OF CATANIA

Instead of telling anecdotes, Alessandro Pluchino, Andrea Rapisarda and Cesare Garofalo, in their article *The Peter Principle Revisited: A Computational Study*, preferred to try a different way of tackling the model in reality. They used a computer simulation of the evolution of the pyramid structure by varying the hypotheses of promotion. Their article revealed astonishing findings, earning them an Ig Nobel Prize in Economics, a parody of the Nobel Prize that rewards the most unusual research. However, their study is nevertheless very serious and the bizarre nature of the results reinforces the thinking and humorous hypotheses developed by Peter.

Definition of a fictitious organisation

Therefore, they created, on a computer program (using Netlogo, a programming language specifically designed for conducive multi-agent simulation to test different aspects of game theory), a fictitious organisation made up of six hierarchical levels (containing 81, 41, 21, 11, 5 and 1 agents respectively). Each agent is characterised by an age ranging from 18 to 60 and a skill level from 1 to 10.

At the beginning of the simulation, ages and skills levels are randomly determined on the basis of the statistical distribution described above.

'NORMAL' STATISTICAL DISTRIBUTION

A statistical distribution gives a strong probability of near-average results – arbitrarily set to 0 on the chart – and an increasingly low probability as we try to get a result that moves away from the top or the bottom. This is considered to be the form of chance that best describes the reality of large samples and, by definition, we find far more average events than exceptional events.

Statistical distribution

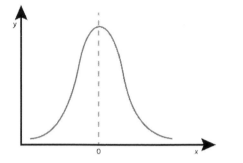

Simulation

Once the initial situation is established, the simulation can begin. In each round of the game, the age of the agents is increased. Each agent who reaches 60 disappears and the gaps are filled by promoting agents from the lower levels. The gaps in the lowest level are filled by adding new agents whose ages and skills are determined randomly.

When an agent changes level, his competence also changes according to the two tested hypotheses:

- **The Peter hypothesis.** The new level of competence is completely random.
- **The common sense hypothesis.** The new level of competence shows a maximum 10% increase or decrease compared with the previous level.

In both cases, it is necessary to measure the overall performance of the system, which corresponds to the average performance of all levels. Note that the more an employee climbs the ladder, the more his individual performance should increase.

Naturally, the question facing researchers is the same one that faces any manager: who should be promoted? For each hypothesis, the researchers tested three types of promotion:

- promoting the best employee;
- promoting the most incompetent employee;
- promoting a randomly selected employee.

Results

Very quickly, the performance of the system reached a point of equilibrium.

Table of the tests and results

Types of promotion	Results according to the Peter hypothesis	Results according to the common sense hypothesis
Promotion of the best employee	Weak efficiency	Increased efficiency
Promotion of the most incompetent employee	Increased efficiency	Weak efficiency
Promotion of a randomly selected employee	Average efficiency	Average efficiency

Under the common sense hypothesis, there is no real surprise. A good overall performance is achieved when the best people are promoted and a poor overall performance when incompetent people are promoted. Random promotion does not have a major impact on overall performance.

On the other hand, if we look at the Peter hypothesis, a surprising conclusion – which is the opposite of that found by the Ig Nobel-winning Italian researchers – is clear: we must promote the incompetent employees. Indeed, if you move a poor worker to a higher level, there is a good chance he will be replaced by someone better than him, the majority of agents being average. In addition to this, the performance of the poor workers will be 'replayed', randomly drawn again, through his reassignment, with a good chance of getting an average result once again. And if the chance results in a bad outcome, he will still proceed to the next round. Thus, promoting the most incompetent employees is the logical conclusion in the Peter hypothesis. Then, as is the case of the common sense hypothesis, chance remains neutral. As for the promotion of the best employees, it works exactly as Peter described: it propels everyone to their level of incompetence, making the overall performance defective.

Conclusion

Therefore, either Peter is right and we can only advise managers to promote the worst employees, or we accept that competence at a higher level is a simple variation of competence at lower levels and promoting the best workers remains the preferred solution.

ADVICE

Overall, Peter approaches the problem in too static and simplistic a manner. Why should the competence for a given position be considered a constant? If the human resource management system in place is effective, regulatory performance measures should be followed by interviews with officials and staff training to increase the efficiency of their work.

Of course, this presents several disadvantages:

- Firstly, we need relevant key performance indicators to determine the quality of work as objectively as possible. In the case of a seller, would be sufficient, for example, to simply measure the number of potential customers who entered the store (more and more shops are installing sensors for this purpose), the amount collected by the seller and the relationship between the two. However, the calculation of performance is more risky when it comes to measuring the quality of work produced by a civil servant or an office worker. Peter himself, when speaking of incompetence, gives the impression that it is based more on a widespread feeling than on specific indicators.
- Secondly, an effective human resource system and training are more difficult to implement and more expensive than simply measuring employee performance and directly promoting the right employee based on past experience.

Whether the Peter hypothesis is true or not, managers may

consider the hierarchy in two opposite ways:

- if each function and the skills related to it are clearly defined, it is much simpler to implement key performance indicators and assess performance;
- if, on the contrary, some uncertainty is deliberately left regarding the tasks that each employee must carry out, it is much easier to relieve a worker of some of the tasks for which he is not competent, but this has a considerable impact on efficiency.

Moreover, it is possible to make workers more mobile by removing the ratchet effect. Demotions are more common than Peter seems to believe.

When the Peter hypothesis does not hold

If the Peter hypothesis is not verified, then the common sense system – which involves promoting the best workers – usually set up by organisations if fully efficient. It has the double advantage of motivating employees to scramble to perform better in the hope of getting a promotion, saving the organisation money on training, as they themselves will make every effort to acquire the skill level required for the superior position.

When the Peter hypothesis holds true

On the other hand, it is much more problematic if the Peter hypothesis proves to be true. If the most incompetent workers are promoted, this should be done discreetly due to the risk of demotivating employees. It is also necessary to focus on financial incentives and refrain from using the promotions system as a reward.

This way of considering and giving promotions has its limitations, since it generates significant costs for the organisation and does not find the person best suited for the position.

Finally, if the Peter hypothesis corresponds to the reality of the organisations and the ratchet effect is as fixed as he believes, the only real solution is to support employees as effectively as possible by measuring the skills needed, motivating them and training them. This costs the organisation much more than if the only competition experienced between employees made them competent at all levels of the hierarchy.

SUMMARY

- The principle developed by Laurence J. Peter and Raymond Hull appears in a satirical work entitled *The Peter Principle* from 1969, a time when businesses, facing a stable and economically sound environment, targeted the growth and development of their structure and therefore inevitably managed promotions.
- The principle is based on the following hypothesis: all organisations promote competent employees until they reach a position in which they cannot perform competently and from which they cannot be removed; the organisation therefore moves towards widespread incompetence.
- The contribution lies mainly with managers who need to know how to manage the movements of their staff in order to improve the overall performance of their organisation. They should, to that end, ensure the development of skills and collective intelligence, because no one is perfect, but a team can be.
- The hypotheses of the model cause controversy, particularly the hypothesis that claims the skills required for a new position are not dependent on those seen in the previous position.
- Other laws, including Parkinson's Law on the natural tendency of organisations to eventually become ineffective, lean in the same direction as the Peter Principle.
- Advice:
  - if the Peter hypothesis does not hold, rely on common sense and promote the best employees;

- if the Peter hypothesis holds true:
  * promote the worst employees without making it known;
  * give financial incentives without changing the employees' role;
  * observe each employee individually and operate movements within the same hierarchical level.

We want to hear from you!
Leave a comment on your online library
and share your favourite books on social media!

FURTHER READING

BIBLIOGRAPHY

- Blary, J-L. (1999) Le principe de Peter. *Lettre d'ADELI*. Volume 36.
- Delahaye, J-P. (2011) Le principe de Peter. *Pour la science*. Volume 407, pp. 82-87.
- Peter, L. J. and Hull, R. (2011) *Le Principe de Peter ou pourquoi tout va toujours mal*. [2nd edition]. Paris: Librairie Générale Française.
- Pluchino, A., Rapisarda, A. and Garofalo, C. (2010) The Peter Principle Revisited: A Computational Study. *Physica A: Statistical Mechanics and its Applications*. 3(389), pp. 467-472. [Online]. [Accessed 18 July 2014]. Available from: <http://arxiv.org/pdf/0907.0455v3.pdf>

ADDITIONAL SOURCES

- *Dilbert* by Scott Adams website: http://www.dilbert.com/

Made in the USA
Middletown, DE
28 September 2019